SZALOWSKI
Sonatina

T0052907

for clarinet and piano

CHESTER MUSIC

à mon cher Ami Ludwik Kurkiewicz

SONATINA

ANTONI SZALOWSKI

I

SZALOWSKI
Sonatina

for clarinet and piano

CHESTER MUSIC

à mon cher Ami Ludwik Kurkiewicz

SONATINA

Clarinet in B♭

ANTONI SZALOWSKI

I

II

Antoni Szalowski (b Warsaw, 1907; d Paris, 1973)studied at the Warsaw Conservatory. His teachers included Sikorski (composition), Lewiecki (piano), and Fitelberg (conducting). In 1931 he went to Paris, where he continued his studies with Boulanger.

The Sonatina for clarinet and piano was composed in 1936, the year he became president of the Association of Young Polish Musicians in Paris.

III